Good N
Down the Street

CW00942626

by

Michael Wooderson

Vicar of Chasetown, diocese of Lichfield

GROVE BOOKS

BRAMCOTE   NOTTS.

CONTENTS

ACKNOWLEDGMENTS

This booklet owes everything to the members of St. Thomas', Aldridge, who have proved that this form of evangelism works. Without them it could never have been written. My special thanks go to Richard Grundy, who designed the cover picture, and Lynette Price, who typed the manuscript.

Michael Wooderson
Vicar of Chasetown,
formerly minister at
St. Thomas' Aldridge
(1973-1981)

First Impression February 1982
ISSN 0144–171X
ISBN 0 907536 18 2

1. INTRODUCTION

Much evangelism among adults today is still
Spasmodic—we make a special effort to gear ourselves up for a parish
mission which may last a fortnight, a week, or just a weekend. All
the outsider needs to do then is to lie low for the required period
of time and he will survive to fight another day, until the next
assault is made in one, two, or three, years' time.

Large-scale—all the churches in a town or area work together on a
'Good News for . . .' campaign, or a high-powered team and a big-
name attraction are invited to lead a mission organized by all the
churches.

Done by successful churches only—those that have a large enough
congregation to have people with the spare time to be involved in
all the preparation needed to do evangelism properly.

Evangelism, for all the talk about it, is therefore the domain of the
minority, whereas it ought to be the privilege of the majority; but that
can only come about if each local church is involved in its own
evangelism all the year round. When this is happening, the 'special
effort' simply provides an occasional boost to an ongoing work; but
what churches have the resources to mount and sustain long-term,
ongoing evangelistic activity?—only the large and successful ones.
Therefore evangelism remains the domain of the minority.

Churches that have considerable resources of manpower may, indeed,
seem to have an advantage over smaller and struggling churches. After
all, they have the capacity to mount large-scale evangelistic operations;
they have the personnel to train up others in the congregation for the
job; they can attract 'big-name' evangelists and preachers who will be
more likely to accept the invitation to speak to hundreds than to tens—
but large churches are in the minority and our country can never be
effectively evangelized by them alone, nor by the faithful band of
itinerant full-time evangelists who periodically descend upon our
towns and cities.

The key to the evangelism of our country lies with the multitude of
smaller congregations which maintain a sometimes flickering witness
in every corner of the land. It is really for them that this booklet is
written, in the hope that they may catch a vision of what God may be
able to do through them when they make evangelism a priority.

Large churches may seem to have all the advantages, but I believe that
the opposite is often the case. In evangelism, the advantage lies with
the smaller church.

If James Kennedy, the instigator of the *Evangelism Explosion* method
of evangelism, had gone to a large and thriving church at Coral Ridge,
he would never have devised the scheme that revolutionized his church

and has been adopted so successfully by many others. Any church with 200-plus members will have problems motivating itself for evangelism. In many cases, the building probably looks comfortably full and it certainly feels that way. There are already too many people for everyone to know everyone else, and the problem will only increase if more people join. No matter what the statistics may say about what a tiny minority of the community they really are, psychologically, it does not feel that way when the church is nearly full. And what if new converts are made and join the church? Their presence may pass almost un-noticed in a large congregation; they will make no measurable impact because they form such a small percentage of the total number. It will be months or years before they are sufficiently well-known to be recognized by most of the congregation. Three couples being converted and joining a congregation of 200-plus will make little visible difference, and so the incentive and impetus for evangelism is greatly reduced, but three couples being converted through the evangelistic activity of a congregation of 20 will be immediately and cheeringly obvious. The impact will be so much greater and the incentive for further evangelism almost irresistible.

Furthermore, large churches have to spend a great deal of energy on internal organization and evangelism can easily become a peripheral activity for the minority, a sort of special interest group, such as the choir or the badminton club. The time and energy of the church leadership may be taken up by the pastoral needs of so many people that evangelism slips further and further down their list of priorities. It is much more difficult for evangelism to have a central place in the life of a large church, except as an occasional spasmodic activity, and it is certainly more difficult to introduce evangelism into a large church where it has been lost sight of.

No, where evangelism is concerned, smaller churches have the advantage every time. If there are less than fifty people in your church, evangelism can become a central and continuous activity of the whole congregation in a way that would be almost impossible to achieve in a large church.

2. PRINCIPLES

The situation

The experiment in evangelism described in these pages began in a situation typical of many all over the country. It was devised and carried out by the minister and congregation of a daughter church on a new estate.

50 years ago Aldridge was a small village with an ancient parish church, a duck-pond and few shops; today the duck pond has vanished for ever and the few shops have been replaced by supermarkets and a shopping precinct. Like many villages with the misfortune to be situated close to large industrial towns and cities, Aldridge—just ten miles north of Birmingham and five miles east of Walsall, in the industrial West Midlands—has become a 'dormitory' town. Its population now tops 18,000, housed in a series of estates, large and small, which have surrounded and overwhelmed the ancient village. Many of the people who live there have moved out from Birmingham or Walsall, or have come to the West Midlands from other parts of the country. The most recent and most extensive phase of building began in the mid-60's and has only just been completed. The parish was alert to the challenge and in 1969 opened St. Thomas's Church Centre, a dual-purpose building, situated right at the heart of the largest estate in the new area. The minister at St. Thomas' has pastoral responsibility for three estates with a total population of about 6,000. The housing includes owner-occupied and council-owned properties (about a 70/30 mix), and ranges from small terraced town houses or council flats and maisonettes to four-bedroomed detached houses and a liberal sprinkling of bungalows. There is therefore a good mix of age groups. However, as in any new area, there is at present a predominance of young families, and this was an important factor in our thinking about evangelistic outreach.

It seemed to us that so many of the traditional methods of evangelism depend on people being enticed out of their homes, either into church premises, or neutral premises, or somebody else's home. This is a grave disadvantage where young families are concerned, as it usually means that only one of the partners can go out—even if both want to! So we felt the need to devise some means of taking the good news of Jesus Christ to them in their homes.

But it really all began with . . .

A chance remark

'I would be interested in finding out more about the Christian faith.' That remark, made to me by one of the mourners after a funeral service, set me thinking.

How does an outsider find out about the Christian faith?

How could that man find out what he wanted to know?

He was not the sort of person who learned by reading books, so there was not much I could leave with him. Would he really find out very much by going to a church service, even if I suggested it? I could possibly call to see him once or twice, but what then?

5

The more I thought about it, the more I began to realize how difficult it must be for someone like that ever to get his questions answered. Whom could he ask? You have to be pretty desperate before you tackle a Christian minister; and talking it over with friends in the pub is usually no more than an exercise in swapping opinions and pooling ignorance.

Where then does such a person go? Has the church got anything practical to offer which does not involve reading books or going to church or joining a church group? all of which put such a person off.

I had to admit that we had nothing, no satisfactory way of meeting the need of someone who was interested in finding out about the Christian faith, but with no church strings attached, and as I reflected further, I was convinced that the man at the funeral was not alone in his interest—that there must be many, many people who would be pleased to have the opportunity of finding out about the Christian faith, as long as it didn't mean being involved with the organised church too closely.

Here was a field ready for harvest and we just were not equipped for the job. We had not got the right tools to hand and we had a largely unskilled workforce.

Some remedy had to be found, so I went in search of one.

Thinking it through

It was at this point, in 1974, that I first came across the work of James Kennedy.[1] I was impressed with what I read. Here was a method of evangelism that was carefully worked out and obviously highly effective, not only in winning people to faith in Jesus Christ but also in building them into the church fellowship and equipping them to witness for Christ. My main misgiving about the approach was that it attempted to do too much in too short a time. It seemed to be asking people to make serious decisions with a minimum of information—one evening's discussion hardly seemed an adequate basis for making an informed decision about following Christ. In my experience, very few people today have sufficient grasp of the most elementary facts about the Christian faith to make more than a superficial response in such a short time. In this respect, the English scene may well differ from the American one. These misgivings apart, James Kennedy's approach struck me as so obviously right in many important respects:

1. Here was a method that mobilized the whole church for evangelism. He had found a way of changing the dream of every church leader into reality. Every member of the church could be involved in the evangelistic task.

2. Here was a method that was built on the concept of learning by doing. It did not require people to go through intensive training programmes before they could be involved. It combined theory with practice in the right proportions.

[1] E. Russell Chandler, *The Kennedy Explosion* (Coverdale, 1972), James Kennedy *Evangelism Explosion* (Tyndale House Publishers, 1970).

6

3. Here was a method that went where people are and took the Good News to them in their homes. So many evangelistic enterprises require people to 'get up out of their seats' and make their way to somebody else's house, or church premises or a tent or a Town Hall, and most people just do not have that sort of motivation.

4. Here was a method that made evangelism a continuous activity and a normal part of the church life. No longer need it be a specialized activity for the few, but a normal activity of the whole body.

If I did not feel happy about some aspects of it, it was up to me to devise some better way of applying the sound principles on which so much of it was based.

As my mind was occupied with these things, our estate was subjected to its periodic visitation from the Jehovah's Witnesses, and reflection on their methods also contributed to our thinking, as well as impressing upon us the urgency of finding an effective means of taking the gospel to the area! Three elements struck us as particularly important.

1. Systematic visiting aimed at stimulating or uncovering interest.

2. Setting up of study groups in people's homes—this is the aim of their visits as the first step towards membership.

3. New converts are immediately trained to go out visiting, giving them no time to become luke-warm.

We felt strongly that we would want to incorporate these elements in any evangelistic scheme we devised.

All the ingredients were not present, but it was a while before they all fitted together in my mind and emerged as the method we have used with great success since 1974.

The method described
The concept is very simple

We would offer anyone who was interested a simple course about the Christian faith. The course would provide material for discussion.[1] It would take place in people's own homes, at their convenience, and would be led by a team of three members of the congregation. It would try to provide sufficient information about Jesus in a simple and consecutive manner to enable people to make a decision about discipleship for themselves. The whole emphasis would be on informality, and discussion would be allowed to range as widely as the hosts required. It would provide a forum in which they could ask the questions that were troubling them, air their grievances about the

[1] See Appendix B and further discussion below.

church, express freely any objections, clear up misunderstandings, and generally sort out for themselves whether Jesus Christ was relevant to their lives or not. Our experience has been that the formula is right and is based on sound principles.

There were, of course, many aspects of it that we were not aware of when we began. It was an experiment of faith that worked beyond our expectations. Fortunately we monitored our progress carefully from the beginning and the following points have emerged from our own reflections over the years and from the questions most frequently asked by those with whom we have had the privilege of sharing our experience.

A. Why a course?
1. *To give the team members confidence*
The prospect of going into someone else's home, even by invitation, for a period of five or six weeks to talk about the Christian faith, filled even our most experienced Christians with great trepidation. Men who were used to open air preaching and door-to-door visiting, trembled at the thought of being exposed to all the questions people would be likely to ask in an ongoing situation where they could not get away with glib answers. A course, however simple, would at least mean that they could prepare in advance for one part of the evening's proceedings, even if the rest would be totally unpredictable! It was a necessary prop in the early days to give us the confidence to start.

2. *To provide essential information*
People must have certain information about Jesus Christ before they are asked to follow him or their last state may end up by being worse than their first. On the whole, people no longer know even the barest facts about the life of Jesus, let alone the heart of the gospel message. They need to be fed a considerable amount of basic information before they are in any position to make a decision for or against Christ. A course enables that information to be imparted in small doses week by week, in a way that people accept as normal.

3. *To ensure progress*
A course, centring as it will on a different topic each week, moves the discussion on quite naturally. Without some such structure, the tendency is to go over the same ground again and again *ad nauseam.* In an unstructured situation, it is very difficult to move people on to new ground. The aim of all evangelism is to move people from the point where they are to a point of commitment to Jesus Christ, and a course enables this progression to be achieved more easily.

4. *To ensure continuity*
A course enables information to be conveyed in a logical order, each week building on the week before, so that it forms a sensible pattern in people's minds, rather than being a haphazard jumble of disconnected facts. People like to know in advance what they are going to discuss the following week and to see that it follows on from what has gone

before. It gives a sense of purpose to the whole exercise. If they wish, there is no reason why the hosts cannot have the material in advance week by week so that they can prepare for the coming session.

B. Why three members in a team?

Are not three people rather a lot to invade one home? is many people's immediate reaction. Are not people put off by the prospect? In our experience this has never been the case. When we first started I made a point of visiting each of the homes that had received a team and asked them specifically for their reactions on this point. All of them (including one elderly widow) said that they would rather have three people come than two. The idea, of course, comes from James Kennedy who sets out his reasons in his book, *Evangelism Explosion.* We tried it a little reluctantly and found that it has so many advantages that we would recommend it as a key factor in this kind of evangelistic enterprise. The advantages are numerous and weighty and are set out below—but in no particular order of importance:

1. *It is a safeguard against scandal*

If you follow the Scriptural pattern of working in pairs, it might not be wise to send someone's husband out with someone else's wife, yet a mixed team is essential if you are going to another couple. A husband and wife team would sometimes be possible, but there are practical difficulties if they have a young family. In our experience, most husbands and wives prefer to work separately in order not to inhibit each other. A team of three makes this possible.

2. *Inexperienced people can learn on the job*

In a team of three, there is always room for one inexperienced or apprehensive member, who gets involved in the work of evangelism to his or her untold benefit. A team leader can take with him or her two other less informed Christians and train them. This obviates the need for lengthy and intensive training courses before people are launched into an evangelistic undertaking. People always comment on how much more they learned going out on a team, than when they received one.

3. *New converts can be used without delay*

A team of three means that people who are converted as a result of the course can be fed into a team almost immediately, going out with one or two of the people who visited them. They are familiar with the course and the way it works and so their enthusiasm to tell others can be channelled immediately in a constructive way. Their knowledge of the bible is extremely limited, their grasp of the complexities of the Christian faith very hazy, but their experience of Christ is new, fresh, and invigorating, and they are invaluable members of a team. The people they go to will relate more closely with them than with the other members of the team, because only a short time before they were in a similar position. They prove what no amount of clever argument can, that the Christian faith is relevant to men and women today, and it works.

4. *It makes linking up with the church much easier*

Although we make it clear to people who invite us that we are not aiming to get them to go to church, in the sense they understand that expression, but to enable them to come to a personal decision about Jesus Christ, nevertheless, if they do come to faith, it is vitally important that they are linked with the fellowship of the church in some way. Integrating new Christians into the fellowship is made much easier by the fact that they get to know three members of the church extremely well over a period of six weeks or so. In a real sense they already feel they belong. The team members will look after them in the early days and introduce them gently to the wider fellowship.

5. *It widens and deepens fellowship among church members*
Being engaged on a challenging undertaking such as this binds the team members together at a deeper level than before. As they pray together and support one another, their understanding of one another and their commitment to one another grows. As the same team never goes out twice but is changed after each course is completed, so the fellowship among church members grows wider and deeper.

6. *It provides a wide range of backgrounds for people to relate to*
We always try to match one member of the team with the people they are going to so that there is an easy relationship from the start, but having three members in a team enables us to build in variety as well. One of the things that people have commented on again and again with appreciation is how different all the people on the team were. Their surprise that this should be so probably reflects the popular misconception that when you become a Christian you lose your individuality and have no opinions of your own. In that way the team is unconsciously removing a barrier to commitment in some people's minds.

7. *It enables teams to be weighted*
In many cases, the degree of interest shown at the outset by the husband and wife will vary, sometimes considerably. One partner may begin by agreeing simply to sit in on the first session having been persuaded by the other. One rather hostile husband sat in on the course to make sure that his wife was not taken in and ended up being converted before the course had finished! If it is the husband who is less interested, the team can be weighted in that direction to include two men and one woman. If it is the wife, then two women and one man. In cases where both are equally interested, any permutation will be acceptable.

8. *The course need not be interrupted through illness etc.*
If one member of the team is ill or unable to come (as may well happen over a six week period) at any time during the course period, the team can still function with two members, thereby ensuring valuable continuity. Too many interruptions would seriously hamper the effectiveness of the course.

9. *It creates an ideal size of group*
As the course is based on informal discussion in a relaxed and intimate atmosphere, a team of three ensures the right group dynamic. It

prevents one-to-one conversations taking over the evening; it gives everyone present the opportunity to contribute without embarrassment, or equally to remain silent without being conspicuous.

From our experience, it is impossible to exaggerate the importance of having three members in a team.

C. Why a six week course?

In the beginning, the length of the course was simply calculated on practical grounds. We needed enough time to build up relationships between the team and our hosts and to impart a modicum of information about the Christian faith, but we did not want to make the course too long or we would put people off. We felt that four weeks would be too short (although some people have adapted our course and used it successfully over the shorter period)[1] and eight weeks might put people off, so we split the difference.

Experience has shown that our estimate was about right. No one has yet refused because he or she could not spare six weeks. Church members also are willing to drop other activities for that length of time in order to go out on a team. We have found that it often takes about three or four weeks before the deeper significance of what is being discussed begins to dawn on people. By then they have usually exhausted their repertoire of excuses for not facing up to the real issues involved, and their relationship with the team members has grown to a point of acceptance and trust. This makes it much easier to lead them on to a point of commitment at the end of the course. For those who do make a commitment, we have added an extra session on the Holy Spirit.

[1] See Appendix A.

3. PRACTICE

A long term strategy

If the approach outlined in chapter 2 is to work effectively, It needs to be part of a carefully thought out evangelistic strategy by the local church. If it is tried simply as a 'good idea' by a few enthusiasts, its effectiveness will be severely limited. It is designed to involve the whole congregation and demands a commitment to a long-term strategy on ongoing evangelism. The enthusiasm of a few may well be the launching-pad for this enterprise, but the long-term goal must be to involve the majority of the congregation in active participation in the evangelistic task. Its proper use will affect every aspect of congregational life in due course, from the provision of small structures to nurture new Christians to the version of the Bible read in church. If it is taken on board as just another form of evangelism to be used alongside those already in use, it will not achieve its full potential. It is because this approach is so all-embracing in its effect, that it is easier to implement in a smaller church which does not have so complex an organization that it cannot be re-structured without great upheaval. When a church is ready to take seriously its responsibility to produce and nurture new Christians and is willing for the changes in church life that this will probably entail, then this approach will enable that task to be fulfilled in a most effective way.

In our situation, it sprang initially from a concern expressed strongly by the Church Council that we were making little impact on the community around us in terms of clear commitment to Christ. It was as we prayed and wrestled with this matter, that the project took shape in our minds, but it was not simply the right tool that we needed; we also needed people to use the tool who were spiritually in the right frame of mind, and it was as we worked together in preparation for outreach into the community that God began to work in our own lives, healing relationships and bringing a fresh commitment to his service and to one another.

Both the people and the tools need to be right if we are to be effective in any evangelistic enterprise, but if we wait until both are perfect, we shall wait for ever. In our experience, it was as we pressed ahead with what we felt strongly needed doing, that God prepared the people he wanted to use.

Launching the project

Once we as a Church Council had formulated a clear policy of embarking on a serious enterprise designed to involve the whole congregation, we set about engaging the widest possible support. All those on the Church Electoral Roll received a letter putting them fully in the picture and encouraging them to be involved in the enterprise.

'Dear . . . . .
For some time now the Church Committee has been concerned that we should be making a wider and greater impact upon the

area as a Christian fellowship than is at present the case. It is very easy for us to get so involved with various spheres of activity, both within the Church and outside it, that we forget our responsibility as Christians to take the good news about Jesus Christ to the many people who have no connection with St. Thomas' or any Christian fellowship.

This autumn we want to make a start to remedy this situation by providing a framework which will enable everyone who wishes to take part in a systematic effort to reach other people with the gospel. The scheme we have in mind is a very simple one which does not demand a vast knowledge of the Bible and the Christian faith before anyone can take part in it. All that is really required is a faith in the Lord Jesus Christ that is real, living and worth passing on.

The impact of the scheme will obviously depend on how many people are willing and able to get involved in it. We hope that you will prayerfully consider whether you can participate. Inevitably there will be some for whom this will be impossible for practical reasons, but we would like to think that everyone will be concerned to pray for this enterprise and keep informed of its progress.'

A series of preparation meetings was arranged and people were encouraged to attend.

'the sessions will be planned to last 1 hour and we hope that you will make the effort to come on one of these days each week whether you intend to become actively involved in the practical side of the scheme or not. We shall not assume that because you attend the preparation classes you are in a position to participate actively in the practical outworking of the scheme. Your attendance would simply be an indication of your interest and prayerful concern and would, of course, enable you to know precisely what the scheme is intended to achieve.'

The response was encouraging. About 25 people attended the preparation sessions, although not all of them would be able to participate actively in the scheme.

We spent a lot of time discussing in detail possible course material already in existence. As we went on, more and more people expressed misgivings about the material and put forward ideas about what should be included until it became obvious that we would have to produce our own. So we had to postpone the proposed starting date while I set about writing the course based on the suggestions of those involved in the preparation sessions. On reflection this was the best thing that could have happened. Producing the material was a valuable part of our preparation, and we always advise churches who are thinking of embarking on a similar scheme to use our material simply as a basis for their own preparation, adapting it for their own situation. We are now in the process of revising our course in the light of an adaptation of our material produced by the late Hugh Silvester for his parish in Manchester, and will be incorporating those elements of presentation and content which improve on our original in the revised course.[1] Every situation demands a slightly different approach and we can always gain fresh insights from one another in this way. The important thing is to have complete confidence in the material you are using, while always looking out for ways of improving it.

When the course material was well under way I convened a meeting of all who had been involved in the preparation sessions. How should we proceed? Our original plan had been to distribute leaflets advertising the course, followed up by a personal visit. But at that meeting so many fears were expressed by those present that they would not be able to cope with the hostility or hard questions they might meet that we had to find another way to start. So we opted for a 'trial run' with fringe members of the congregation.[2]

During the 'trial run' more than one team was in action on the same evening so that we could meet afterwards to compare notes and deal with any problems that may have arisen, whether practical or theological. These de-briefing sessions were immensely valuable in the early stages.

The course (A copy is to be found in Appendix B)
The basic course consists of six sessions, with an extra study on the Holy Spirit for those who make a profession of faith. The first session is really just an ice-breaker, and in some ways is the most difficult of all to lead. The brief notes accompanying each session are for the benefit of the team members. They give some indication of the direction in which the study should proceed and the main thrust of the passages chosen for discussion. The 'Commitment' section in the notes on Session 6 is pure James Kennedy and for a more detailed explanation of it you would need to consult his book, *Evangelism Explosion.* It is intended to be a helpful model and not to be used inflexibly! This is the point at which team leaders need most help and where they feel the greatest resistance within themselves. 'Popping the question' in this context, as in the romantic, may take a lot of courage. This is something that can only be overcome with prayer and experience. The temptation to avoid putting the question may sometimes be almost overwhelming and there will be innumerable 'good reasons' why it is not possible. However, for the sake of the people we go to, it is vitally important that they have the opportunity of declaring their position. More than once our teams have asked people whether they are ready to commit their lives to Christ expecting a negative reply, only to be surprised. Even where the team are convinced that a person is already a Christian, it is important that he or she is encouraged actually to say so. Paul's words in Romans 10.9-10 stress the importance of expressing our faith to

[1] See Appendix B.
[2] See p.17 'Finding the homes'.

others:
'. . . if you confess with your lips that Jesus is Lord, and believe in your heart that God raised him from the dead, you will be saved. For man believes with his heart and so is justified, and he confesses with his lips and so is saved.'

It cannot be stressed too strongly that Scripture passages are not intended to be 'proof texts'. They are reference points for the team members who are expected to provide a background and context for them. They provide a scriptural framework within which discussion can take place. As so many people outside the church have never read any part of the New Testament they provide basic information which is designed to stimulate interest and discussion as well as presenting the challenge of Jesus Christ. Our aim is to create a forum in which open, honest debate and discussion can take place, so that people can decide for themselves whether the Christian faith is true and relevant to them. The amount of Scriptural material included in each session is deliberately small—it could be looked at in 20 minutes or half an hour—although in a 'non-book culture' it would probably need to be even smaller (see Appendix A).

The course is designed to be used with the Good News Bible, and the page numbers refer to the paperback edition of the New Testament published by the Bible Society/Fount. We opted for this translation because

—it is easy to read and understand.
—it is attractively produced
—it is relatively cheap
—it has individual Gospel portions

It is very important that the people who invite a team are not made to feel at a disadvantage, or embarrassed by their ignorance of the Bible. We therefore insist that our team members work only from the Good News Bible and have with them only the same books as their hosts. In the first two sessions, for example, the team will take with them only the individual Gospel portions of Luke and John. We are not out to impress people with our superior knowledge or expertise but to encourage them to explore for themselves the truth of the claims of Jesus Christ. As everyone works from the same book, references can be given by page numbers instead of chapter and verse—a considerable advantage, as finding the place by chapter and verse is a strange procedure to the uninitiated. We supply all the materials to our hosts free of charge and they are invited to keep them at the end of the course. A complete pack consists of:

1 Good News Luke
1 Good News John
1 Good News New Testament
1 *Power to live by* (notes on John, publ. Scripture Union)
1 *Verdict on the empty tomb* (Val Grieve, publ. Falcon)
1 *Journey into Life* (Norman Warren, publ. Falcon)
1 *The Way Ahead* (Norman Warren, publ. Falcon)
1 Copy of course material

Each person we visit will receive his or her own set of materials. We use them as follows:

> Session 1—after the preliminaries are over, 1 John's Gospel, 1 Luke's Gospel plus study outline for Session 1 to each person present. When the brief study is ended, just before you leave, one copy of *Power to live by* with an explanation of what it is and how to use it.
>
> Session 2—Outline for study 2 for each person present.
>
> Session 3—1 Good News New Testament plus study outline 3.
>
> Session 4—study outline 4 and, at conclusion of study, *Verdict on the empty tomb.*
>
> Session 5—study outline 5.
>
> Session 6—study outline 6 and, at end of course, *Journey into life.* If there is a definite commitment, leave *The Way Ahead* as well.

Note about the 'Preparation for next session'
> This is not 'homework' and people should be reassured that this is the case. The questions at the end of Session 1, for example, are only intended to set people thinking about the subject for the following week. There is not meant to be a 'correct answer' that you can mark (see notes on Session 2). We have always stressed to our team members that they must resist the urge to 'correct' erroneous views at this stage—rather should they let the Scriptures do their own work as they go through the Biblical material with their hosts. At the end of the session, they can then be asked whether they have revised their opinion in the light of what they have learned. In that way people are not made to look ignorant or feel foolish, and the Holy Spirit through the Scriptures can do his own work.

Follow up

This is in many ways already built into the scheme.[1] However, most new Christians will benefit from a more structured introduction to the church family. This is more easily achieved, at least in the early stages of setting up such a project, if the teams operate within set periods, say January-March, September-October. (In our experience, people who are interested in receiving a team do not mind waiting a few months until they can begin the course). The new Christians resulting from the teams' activities can then meet together in groups for further instruction before being fully integrated into the church fellowship.

When we began the scheme at St. Thomas', like many small churches we had a mid-week meeting for Bible study and prayer to which a few keen, longstanding Christians came. This was obviously totally unsuitable for receiving six to eight new Christians. So in the early stages we re-organized our mid-week meeting. The longstanding

[1] See pp.9-10, section 4.

Christians continued to meet in one room for the first part of the evening. The new Christians met as a group in another room for a separate six-part course of instruction building on what they had learnt from the initial course in their homes. They were joined by the no. 2 member of each team that had gone out to their homes, who thereby provided a pastoral link. As they also took it in turns to lead the group study and discussion this gave them further valuable experience in preparation for team leadership. For the last 30 minutes of the evening the two groups met together for a time of sharing and informal prayer. By the end of the six weeks the two groups were then in a position to integrate and share a common programme.

As the scheme begins to take effect and the church grows in numbers a system of local area house groups is probably the most effective method of long-term nurture for new church members.[1] But it is still important for the new Christians to meet together as a group before they join any house group.

The sharing of common experience is an enormous help and encouragement to them. They learn that they are not alone in what has happened and is happening to them, they build one another up in the faith, and grow in confidence and understanding of their new-found faith. It also means that when they join a house group, the group has had time to prepare for them and knows just what ground they have covered.

Finding the homes
Perhaps the most frequent question we are asked is 'How do you persuade people to let a team of three strangers into their homes to discuss the Christian faith?'

I am fully aware that it may have something to do with my own ability to persuade them, rather than put them off, but I do not feel that that is the whole story.[2] Certainly in the early years of setting up such a scheme the full involvement of the minister is important, and without it the scheme would probably not get off the ground, but there will be members of the congregation quite capable of carrying on the scheme once it is launched.

Our experience was quite simply that when as a church we were ready for this form of evangelism, then the openings came. I am convinced that that would be the case in most other places too. In point of fact, we started by trying out the course on people who were already connected with the church through the monthly Family Service. When we were ready to start, we were rather apprehensive about how the course would work in practice, so I approached various people who would not be well known by the team members, explained to them what we were proposing to do and asked them if they would be willing to act as guinea pigs so that we could train ourselves. We had sufficient people willing to go out for us to field five teams and none of the

[1] See Grove Pastoral Series No. 3—David Prior *Sharing Pastoral Care in the Parish.* (1980).
[2] See Appendix A.

homes I approached refused to help us with our experiment. In fact they went out of their way to co-operate. We were greatly encouraged by people's response to the course; both team members and hosts had obviously thoroughly enjoyed it and learnt a great deal as a result. There was the added bonus for us of having one couple converted, one husband married to a Christian converted, and one elderly widow having her faith strengthened and deepened. In two homes, there was no positive commitment, although in one case the wife became a Christian six months later. In every case the experience was such a good one that the relationships with the church were strengthened.

After this trial run, our original plan was to work systematically through our area advertising the course with leaflets and personal visits. However, that did not prove necessary; through normal pastoral contacts, baptism enquiries, etc. we suddenly began to find people expressing an interest in finding out more about the Christian faith and they needed very little persuasion to invite one of our teams into their home.

I always made it very clear to them that we were not wanting to get them to go to church, and our teams were strictly instructed not to invite people to do so. Any initiative in that direction must come from them and not us. I also re-assured them that we would put no pressure on them and if they were unhappy in any way, they only had to say and the team would stop coming. As the meetings were in their home, they had every right to ask us to leave if they wished. It has always been our aim to involve both husband and wife, however reluctant one of the partners may be at the start, and we would certainly not go ahead if one partner objected. Most people are afraid either of being 'got at' or of being made to look ignorant and if they can be reassured on those two counts, they can usually be persuaded at least to sit in on the proceedings for the first week. Very few then opt out in our experience. As the first contact with a home usually comes through the wife, this has meant that by working in this way we have seen many men converted who otherwise may never have come near the church.

People who are interested in the course are given a leaflet set out as follows:

'For your information
We have designed a simple course about the Christian faith which has in mind anyone who is interested in sorting out for themselves whether it is true and relevant to the world today. It consists of an introduction and five sessions based on the life and teaching of Jesus Christ. During the course we look at various passages in the New Testament in an easy-to-read modern English version which we provide. We hope that these passages will stimulate discussion as well as give information about what Jesus actually said and did. In our experience, many people have rather hazy ideas about these things—all they can recall are snippets of half-correct information from their R.I. lessons at school, or perhaps from what they have heard on television or the occasional visit to church. Many people, too, have lots of

unanswered questions and welcome the opportunity to discuss them with someone who may be able to point them towards an answer.

All the people who have used this course have commented on how helpful it is in these ways.

We will send you a team of three people, who are ordinary members of the congregation, to work through the course with you. They may not be able to answer all your questions on the spot, but they will be able to share with you what they have found to be true about the Christian faith in their own experience and will always try to find a satisfactory answer to your queries.

The team will come to your home on any evening that is convenient to you and will stay as long or short time as you want them to.

If any problems arise, please do not hesitate to contact . . .'

When all the arrangements have been made, the team leader will usually call at the home and introduce himself/herself before the first meeting just to put the hosts at ease about who is coming.

The course is particularly attractive to people with young families who find it difficult to do much together in the evening unless it is in the home environment, but we have found that its appeal covers all ages and circumstances. We have used it with miners and milkmen as well as schoolteachers and solicitors, with bank managers and businessmen, firemen, shop assistants, engineers, draughtsmen, factory hands, salesmen, senior citizens and housewives.

The secret of this approach is that people really are interested in other people and what makes them tick. It is that which explains the popularity of 'Parkinson' and 'This is your life'. It is the team who communicate the reality of Christ by the sort of people they are as well as what they share of their own faith in the course of the meetings.

Finding the Leaders
Who was going to lead the teams? No-one was exactly jumping to volunteer; but I knew that there were five people quite capable of doing the job. They were all Christians of long standing with a competent knowledge of the Bible and the Christian faith. They had no prior experience of doing anything like this. Open-air preaching, door-to-door visiting, teaching in Sunday School, these they had experience of; but the thought of six whole evening face-to-face with complete strangers who might ask anything filled them with great trepidation. They would have liked me to go out with them first time round, or if that were not possible, at least a course in apologetics, followed by a course in personal evangelism, followed by a course in anything to put off the moment of starting. But I knew that they were perfectly competent for the task—all they really needed was the courage to start. Courses would only confuse them, or provide them with pat answers

that people do not want. They would learn more from having to wrestle with the questions people posed and searching for answers than if they were supplied with 'answers' in advance. Six weeks of dialogue with people seeking for a meaning to their lives would be worth six months of courses. If they came up against any problems they could always consult me. I made it as clear as I could that I saw my role as that of a resource person.

My reluctance to lead a team myself, and my refusal to do so when we were getting the scheme started, sprang from a fear of inhibiting either the team members or the people they went to. The presence of a clergyman, however 'unclerical' he may be, tends to have that effect. He is, after all, the 'professional'. Some people would still regard him with a certain amount of respect and would be reticent to express their true feelings, and many more would be afraid of showing their ignorance about the Christian faith in front of an expert. In rare cases only have I felt free to go out on a team—and my own track record is not particularly impressive from the angle of results!

The clergyman also inhibits the other team members in an important way. If he is going to be present they will rely on him to 'field' the difficult questions and therefore they will rely less on the Holy Spirit to give them the words to speak.

In the early stages of setting up such a scheme the onus of team leadership will inevitably fall on the few. It is therefore vitally important that they are released from other responsibilities so that they are not over-burdened. In a smaller church all the leaders tend to be tied up in several jobs. We overcame this particular difficulty by organizing our evangelistic outreach into two periods of the year. People who expressed interest in inviting a team would be told that they would be starting in a particular month (sometimes it would be as much as three months ahead). We would then start all the teams during the same week, and for the duration of the course we would close down all midweek activities. Evangelism was given absolute priority on leaders' time during that period. If there was a Church Council meeting they were not expected to attend; and there would be no Bible Study or prayer meeting, so that they weren't made to feel guilty about missing it!

Within a couple of years the load begins to ease as new leaders emerge from within the scheme.[1]

[1] See chart p.21.

4. CONCLUSION

The long-term effects of this approach on the life of the congregation are far-reaching.

In the six years from March 1975 to March 1981, we have used the course with 200 individuals (that includes 63 couples) sending out 89 teams and involving 120 different members of the congregation. As our current Electoral Roll stands at about 150, it will be seen that a high percentage of the congregation have now experienced being part of a team and a considerable proportion have become church members directly as a result of a visit from one of our teams. We have now reached the point where people expect to go out on a team at regular intervals and are very disappointed if they are deprived of the opportunity for any length of time. I have been approached on many occasions by people asking me to try and fit them into a team. People have come to regard evangelism as a normal and natural part of their Christian life.

How effective the course has been may be judged from the figures below:

Of the 200 different people who have received a team:
> 5 failed to complete the course
> 15 were already Christians
> 136 made a commitment to Christ
> 4 have made commitment since
> 40 made no positive decision

The lapse rate of those who made commitments is quite low, although we could wish it were lower. Just ten have failed to get really involved in the life of the church, but we are still in touch with them and they come to services, occasionally. Of those who made no commitment likewise many are still in touch with the church.

This approach also encourages people to grow rapidly in their Christian faith and gives them opportunities to take leadership responsibilities instead of becoming one of God's frozen people. The following chart shows the sort of progress such a person might make:

	Time Scale	
	Jan.-Feb.	Visited by team, made a commitment
	Mar.-Apr.	Welcome Group with other new Christians
	May-June	No. 3 in a team
Two Years	Sept.-Dec.	Further instruction
	Jan.-Feb.	No. 2 in a team
	Mar.-Dec.	House Fellowship Group
	Jan.-Feb.	No. 1 in a team

APPENDIX A: A SUCCESSFUL ADAPTATION

We are a Methodist congregation of some 50 years standing. Our area is suburban, but not modern and middle class; rather, it is a mixture of pre-war council houses and flats, with some old and some newer owner-occupied housing. We were not a new church beginning to establish itself but a once strong church slowly but steadily in decline over a number of years. The morning congregation had shrunk to around 40 adults, with the 15-40 age group almost totally unrepresented; very few of the families of children in Sunday School had a living church link. The evening service was on the point of being discontinued through lack of support. There were no house groups; and the main activity of the church was keeping going the worship programme and the buildings.

Some of the church members were indeed concerned at the plight of the church for a variety of reasons, both sacred and secular, godly and selfish. The main need seemed to be to ground this concern in the will and purpose of God for his church and to channel it in the right direction. A start was made by facing the church with the uncomfortable truth that there were in the future only two choices: either the church must begin to grow, or it would die within 30 years when the last of the present members died. Furthermore, if the church was to grow, the congregation would have to go out with the gospel, as our Lord commanded; to continue complaining that 'they won't come to church any more' was simply disobedience to our Lord's commission. People gradually began to see that the need was for evangelism, but they were unsure about exactly how to do it and hesitant to start.

It was at this point, in 1980, that I approached several people individually to talk to them about the scheme described in this booklet and asked them if they would be willing to try it. Their two main fears about evangelism were:

1. that they would have to contact people out of the blue (perhaps on the street, or by door-knocking).
2. that they would not know what to say.

When they learned that they would be asked to visit people who had already been contacted and were actually looking forward to their coming, and that they would be following a carefully programmed course of study, their two main fears all but disappeared and they were willing to give it a try. They were further encouraged by knowing that everyone would be carefully prepared before going. I felt that the course material as it stood would not suit our situation, so I re-wrote, shortened and simplified it. Our preparation included studies of the course itself, sermons and house group discussions on common objections to the Christian faith, an evening's discussion with a member of another church who had been out on such teams a number of times, and as much prayer as we could muster.

None of those who eventually went out had done anything like this before. None knew quite what to expect, or whether they would be any good at it. But they all went in a spirit of willing obedience to see if they could serve Christ in this way.

Over the past 18 months the results have been most encouraging. For those who have gone out, it has brought a sharper understanding of the Christian gospel, a new faith in the power of the living God to bring people back to himself, and an increased confidence in themselves.

For those to whom we went, it has brought new faith in Christ, (yes, people were converted!) and even among those who chose not to commit themselves to Christ it has brought a greater understanding of the facts and the issues involved, and a new respect for the church.

For the church as a whole it has brought a fresh encouragement, as new people are seen in church and testimonies are given in services. And in the community it has aroused interest and comment (people talk!); not long after we started we had a request from a relation of one of the families to whom we had sent a team: 'Could you send me a team too?' That has been our experience. The fire, once started, has spread far more quickly and burned hotter than my meagre faith in the Holy Spirit ever led me to expect.

APPENDIX B: COURSE MATERIAL (AS REVISED 1981)

Session 1: Jesus—the key to understanding
The key to understanding the Christian faith is Jesus Christ. Most of the reliable information we have about Jesus is to be found in the Bible.

1. *To understand Jesus we must read the Bible*
   Luke tells us why he wrote his gospel:
   Luke chapter 1 verses 1-4 (p.1)
   - ● those who saw
   - ● carefully studied
   - ● orderly account
   - ● the full truth

2. *The Bible helps us to believe in Jesus*
   Knowing about Jesus, important though it is, is only a first step.
   John explains why he wrote his gospel: John chapter 20 verses 30-31 (p.62)

* * * *

Preparation for next session   **Who was Jesus?**
How would you describe Jesus?
   —a good man?.............................
   —a perfect man? ....
   —a religious maniac? ....
   —a holy man?..............................
   —an astronaut?.............................
   —a great religious teacher?.................
   —God? ....
How do you know?

Notes on Session 1
Your first visit is very important. By the time you leave, the people you have visited should have perceived:
1. that you are genuinely interested in them as people
2. that you are perfectly normal people, like themselves
3. that Jesus Christ means a lot to you.
You need to spend most of this session getting to know the people you are visiting and telling them about yourselves. The very brief study should be used to round off the evening.

From the general course of conversation or by direct question you will want to find out the following:
   —Have you ever had any Church contact?
   —How long ago and for what reasons did they lose touch with the Christian church?
   —How did they come to invite a team?
   —Have they got any particular problems: e.g. bereaved, lonely, housebound, etc.?
Before you visit, pray (preferably as a team).
While you visit, relax. (The Holy Spirit is in charge)
End on a note of encouragement and expectation.
Leave any relevant literature. Arrange next visit.

[N.B. As the notes are only intended for team members it is advisable to produce them on a separate sheet. They will fit easily on one side of an A5 sheet, as will each session outline.]

Session 2:   Who was Jesus?
A. *What people said about him*
   1. Luke 11 verses 14-15 (p.42)
   2. Luke 4.41 (p.15)
   3. John 8.48 (p.28)
   4. John 9.30-33 and 10.19-21 (p.31 and 33)
   5. Luke 23.13-16 (p.81)
   6. John 1.43-49 (p.5)

B. *What Jesus said about himself*
   1. John 5.1-21 (p.14)
   2. John 6.25-44 (p.19)
   3. John 14.1-11 (p.44)

C. *What his disciples said about him*
   1. Before his death John 6.66-69 (p.21)
   2. After his death John 20.26-28 (p.62)

* * * *

Preparation for next session
What would you say were the most important things Jesus did?
   1. Taught people about God
   2. Performed miracles
   3. Died on the cross
   4. Lived a perfect life as an example to us
Arrange in order of importance.

Notes on Session 2
1. Check that your hosts have done the preparation work.
2. Do not attempt to correct their answers at this point or pass any detailed comment on them. Leave any discussion until after the study.

Section A is designed to show that people reacted to Jesus in a variety of ways.

Passages 1 and 2 stand in striking contrast. The demons recognize Jesus for who he is, while the crowd are divided in their opinions.

Passage 3 comes at the end of the debate Jesus had with the Jews in which he claimed to come from God (John 8.42). They dismissed his claim as madness.

Passage 4 contrasts the matter-of-fact faith of the blind man with the desperate attempts of the Jewish leaders to discredit the miracle Jesus had performed.

Passage 5 gives the opinion of someone who could give a more objective assessment of Jesus.

Passage 6 shows a sceptical Jew confronted with Jesus and changing his mind.

GOOD NEWS DOWN THE STREET

Section B covers just 3 passages where Jesus makes unmistakable claims to be God.

Passage 1 follows a healing miracle. Verses 17-18 are the key ones.
Passage 2 follows Jesus' feeding of the 5000.
Passage 3 comes from Jesus' last conversation with his disciples where he tells them that he is soon going to leave them.

Section C simply pinpoints 2 notable confessions of faith: that of Peter and that of Thomas.

Conclusion. A word of personal testimony might not be out of place at this point.

_____

Session 3

What Jesus did

1. *Jesus did miracles*
   Luke 7.11-23 (p.168)

4. *Jesus died on the cross*
   a. What did Jesus regard as his life's work?
      John 6.39-40 (p.252)

2. *Jesus taught people*
   Matthew 7.28-29 (p.20)
   John 7.14-16 (p.254)
   Matthew 7.24-26 (p.20)

         John 10.10b (p.264)
         Mark 10.45 (p.120)

   b. He knew he had to die
      Mark 8.31-33 (p.113)

3. *Jesus lived a perfect life*
   Hebrews 4.14-16 (p.550)
   Hebrews 7.26-27 (p.554)
   1 Peter 2.22-24 (p.582)

         Mark 9.30-32 (p.116)
         John 3.14-15 (p.241)
         John 12.32-33 (p.272)

   c. What did his death achieve?
      Romans 5.6-11 (p.388)
      2 Corinthians 5.14-15 (p.453)
      Colossians 1.20-22 (p.503)

               *   *   *   *

Preparation for next session
Read Luke chapter 24 (p.299)

    John chapter 20 and 21.1-14 (p.291)

Notes on Session 3

1. *Jesus did miracles.* Don't let this one develop into a red herring. The importance of the miracles, as the passage makes clear, was that they were sure signs that Jesus was in fact the Messiah as John the Baptist had announced (John 1.29-34).

2. *Jesus taught people*
   They listened because he spoke with such authority; but Jesus' teaching is not just to be listened to but to be put into practice. It's not for theoretical discussion or mental assent, but for action.

3. *Jesus lived a perfect life*
   His sinlessness is another pointer to his divinity. Because Jesus was perfect, he was able to link men to God once more. The job of the priest in the Old Testament was to act as a go-between, linking sinful man to a sinless God, a task he could never properly fulfil.

4. *Jesus died on the cross*
   This last section of the study is the most important. Try not to spend too long on the first three. Follow the example of the Gospel writers who concentrate heavily on the last week of Jesus' life.

Recommended reading for team members:
Understanding the death of Jesus by John Eddison (published by Scripture Union). Especially chapter 4.

Session 4:

Jesus was raised from the dead

1. *His tomb was empty*
   Luke 24.1-3 (p.229)
   John 20.1-10 (p.291)

   How can it be explained?
   —Body stolen? see Matthew 27.62-66 (p.85)
                          Matthew 28.11-15 (p.86)
   —Not really dead? see John 19.31-34 (p.290)
                           Mark 15. 42-45 (p.141)

2. *He was seen alive again*
   Luke 24 (p.299)

   1 Corinthians 15.3-8 (p.440)

3. *His disciples were changed*
   Before
   Luke 22.54-62 (p.223)
   Luke 24.13-21 (p.230)
   John 20.19 (p.290)

   After
   Acts 4.1-22 esp. verse 13 (p.308)
   Acts 5.27-39 (p.313)

4. *His resurrection confirms his claims*
   John 2.18-22 (p.240)
   Luke 9.21-22 (p.178)

   Luke 18.31-34 (p.209)